TRAVEL DIARY

Scotland

TravelEgg

IMPORTANT INFORMATION

Name:

Email address:

Tel:

Address:

Important Medical Information

Blood type:

Medication:

CONTENTS

We hope you enjoy this journal. It has plenty of space to record details of your trip, and some useful information to help you plan your journey.

ENJOY YOUR TRIP

THINGS TO DO

Edinburgh Castle
Royal Botanic Gardens Edinburgh
The National Museum of Scotland
Riverside Museum
Mull Museum
Kelvingrove Art Gallery and Museum
Real Mary King's Close
Eilean Donan Castle
Melrose Abbey
Creetown Gem Rock Museum
Callendar House and Park

Edinburgh Zoo
Glasgow Cathedral
Pittencrieff Park
Ben Nevis
Falls of Shin
Calderglen Country Park
Stirling Castle
Strathclyde Country Park
Corrigal Farm Museum
Duthie Park
Vogrie Country Park
Dean Castle
Victoria Park

PLACES TO EAT

Tower Restaurant (Edinburgh)

National Museum, Chambers Street, EH1 1JF

The Kitchin

78 Commercial St, Edinburgh EH6 6LX

The Witchery by the Castle

352 Castlehill, Edinburgh EH1 2N

Wildfire

192 Rose St, Edinburgh EH2 4AZ

The Grog & Gruel (Fort William)

66 High St, Fort William PH33 6AD

Crannog Seafood Restaurant

The Waterfront, Fort William PH33 6DB

Ubiquitous Chip (Glasgow) 12 Ashton Ln, Glasgow G12 8SJ
Qua Italian Restaurant 68 Ingram St, Glasgow G1 1EX
Number 16 Restaurant 16 Byres Rd, Glasgow G11 5JY
Bread Meats Bread 104 St Vincent St, Glasgow G2 5UB
The Dores Inn (Inverness) B862, Dores, Inverness IV2 6TR
The Riverside Restaurant 10 Bank St, Inverness IV1 1QY
The Mustard Seed Restaurant 16 Fraser St, Inverness IV1 1DW

POSTCARD LIST

Name:
Address:

Name:
Address:

Name:
Address:

Name:

Address:

Name:

Address:

Name:

Address:

Name:

Address:

PACKING LIST

✓	**Tickets**
	Passport
	Money

CLOTHES SIZE

Children's Shoe Sizes

UK	EUROPE	US	Japan
4	20	4½ or 5	12 ½
4 ½	21	5 or 5½	13
5	21 or 22	5½ or 6	13 ½
5 ½	22	6	13½ or 14
6	23	6½ or 7	14 or 14½
6 ½	23 or 24	7 ½	14½ or 15
7	24	7½ or 8	15
7 ½	25	8 or 9	15 ½
8	25 or 26	8½ or 9	16
8 ½	26	9½	16 ½
9	27	9½ or 10	16 ½ or 17
10	28	10½ or 11	17 ½
10½ or 11	29	11½ or 12	18
11 ½	30	12½	18 or 18 ½
12	31	13	19 or 19 ½
12 ½	31	13 or 13½	19 ½ or 20
13	32	1	20
13 ½	32 ½	1 ½	20 ½
1	33	1½ or 2	21
2	34	2½ or 3	22

Children's Clothing Sizes

UK	EUROPE	US	Australia
12m	80cm	12-18m	12m
18m	80-86cm	18-24m	18m
24m	86-92cm	23-24m	2
2-3	92-98cm	2T	3
3-4	98-104cm	4T	4
3-5	104-110cm	5	5
5-6	110-116cm	6	6
6-7	116-122cm	6X-7	7
7-8	122-128cm	7 to 8	8
8-9	128-134cm	9 to 10	9
9-10	134-140cm	10	10
10-11	140-146cm	11	11
11-12	146-152cm	14	12

Women's Shoe Sizes

UK	EUROPE	US	Japan
3	35 ½	5	22 ½
3 ½	36	5 ½	23
4	37	6	23
4 ½	37 ½	6 ½	23 ½
5	38	7	24
5 ½	39	7 ½	24
6	39 ½	8	24 ½
6 ½	40	8 ½	25
7	41	9 ½	25 ½
7 ½	41 ½	10	26
8	42	10 ½	26 ½

Women's Clothes Sizes

UK	US	Japan	France / Spain	Germany	Italy	Australia
6/8	6	7-9	36	34	40	8
10	8	9-11	38	36	42	10
12	10	11-13	40	38	44	12
14	12	13-15	42	39	46	14
16	14	15-17	44	40	48	16
18	16	17-19	46	42	50	18
20	18	19-21	48	44	52	20

Men's Shoe Sizes

UK	EUROPE	US	Japan
6	38 ½	6 ½	24 ½
6 ½	39	7	25
7	40	7 ½	25 ½
7 ½	41	8	26
8	42	8 ½	27 ½
8 ½	43	9	27 ½
9	43 ½	9 ½	28
9 ½	44	10	28 ½
10	44	10 ½	28 ½
10 ½	44 ½	11	29
11	45	12	29 ½

Men's Suit / Coat / Sweater Sizes

UK / US / Aus	EU / Japan	General
32	42	Small
34	44	Small
36	46	Small
38	48	Medium
40	50	Large
42	52	Large
44	54	Extra Large
46	56	Extra Large

Men's Pants / Trouser Sizes (Waist)

UK / US	Europe
32	81 cm
34	86 cm
36	91 cm
38	97 cm
40	102 cm
42	107 cm

PHRASES

English	Scots Gaelic	French	Spanish
Hello	halò	Bonjour	Hola
Goodbye	mar sin leat	Au revoir	Adiós
Yes	tha	Oui	Sí
No	chan eil	Non	No
Please	mas e do thoil e	S'il-vous-plaît	Por favor
Thank you	Tapadh leat	Merci	Gracias
Excuse me	Gabh mo leisgeul	Excusez-moi	Perdón
How much	Cia mheud	Combien	Cuánto
My name is	Is e m' ainm	Mon nom est	Mi nombre es
Where is	Càite a bheil	Où est	Dónde está
The bank	am banca	La banque	El banco
The toilet	an taigh beag	Les toilettes	El baño

PHRASES

Italian	German	Japanese	Mandarin
Ciao	Hallo	Kon'nichiwa	Ni hao
Arrivederci	Auf Wiedersehen	Sayonara	Zaijian
Si	Ja	Hai	Shi de
No	Nein	Ie	Meiyou
Per favore	Bitte	Onegaishimasu	Qing
Grazie	Vielen Dank	Arigato	Xiexie
Mi scusi	Entschuldigung	Sumimasen	Duoshao
Quanto	Wie viel	Ikura	Wo de mingzi shi
Io mi chiamo	Mein Name ist	Watashinonamaeha	Nali
Dov'è	Wo ist	Doko ni aru	Yinhang
La banca	Die Bank	Ginko	Yinhang
Il bagno	Die Toilette	Toire	Cesuo

TRIP DIARY

DAY 1

DAY 2

DAY 3

DAY 4

DAY 5

DAY 6

DAY 7

DAY 8

DAY 9

DAY 10

DAY 11

DAY 12

DAY 13

DAY 14

DAY 15

DAY 16

DAY 17

DAY 18

DAY 19

DAY 20

DAY 21

DAY 22

DAY 23

DAY 24

DAY 25

DAY 26

DAY 27

DAY 28

DAY 29

DAY 30

MEMORIES

&

Name:
Address:
Tel:
email:

Name:
Address:
Tel:
email:

Name:
Address:
Tel:
email:

| Name: |
| Address: |
| Tel: |
| email: |

| Name: |
| Address: |
| Tel: |
| email: |

| Name: |
| Address: |
| Tel: |
| email: |

| Name: |
| Address: |
| Tel: |
| email: |

NOTES

www.ingramcontent.com/pod-product-compliance
Lightning Source LLC
LaVergne TN
LVHW080908060725
815431LV00025BA/855